Coral Reefs

PIONEER EDITION

By Peter Winkler

CONTENTS

CORAL REEFS

Cities in the Sea

What animals make the biggest homes? They might be tiny ocean animals.

Many animals make homes. But some build whole cities. That is what **coral polyps** do. These animals build cities in the ocean.

Coral Building

Coral polyps are big builders. Yet they are small animals. Many are less than an inch long. They are shaped like tubes.

One end of the polyp has hooks. These help the polyp stay in one place. The other end has a mouth and arms. These let the polyp find food.

Coral polyps have hard skeletons. The skeletons are made of rock called limestone. When a polyp dies, the limestone skeleton stays behind.

Young polyps soon hook onto it. They live there. Then they die. Over time, the limestone skeletons pile up. They form a **coral reef.**

BY PETER WINKLER

Australia's Great Barrier Reef

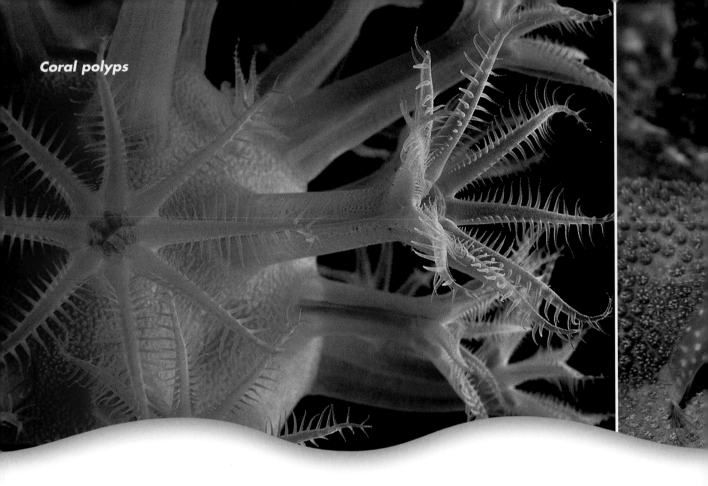

Coral polyps

Supersize Cities

Coral grows in all shapes and sizes. Some coral looks like tiny trees. Some is shaped like cabbage. Some looks like a giant brain!

Coral can form small reefs. It can form big ones too. The largest coral reef is the Great Barrier Reef. It is off the coast of Australia. The Great Barrier Reef covers 135,000 square miles. That is nearly the size of New Mexico!

Scientists think of coral reefs as underwater cities. That is because reefs are homes to many animals.

Colorful Crowds

Who lives in reefs? Crabs and eels do. So do octopuses, sharks, and turtles.

Many kinds of fish also live there. Tiny blennies hide among the coral. Parrotfish eat the limestone.

Plants also grow in coral reefs. Some of the brightest are tiny **algae** (AL jee). These plants are bright red, green, blue, or yellow.

Algae make reefs colorful. They live inside coral polyps. Polyps have clear bodies. So the algae's colors show through.

Blenny

Colorful fish and coral

Cup coral eating fish

Food, Fun, and More

People do not live in coral reefs. But reefs help us in big ways.

Coral reefs give us food. We eat lots of fish from reefs. In fact, coral reefs feed millions of people.

People have to catch and sell the animals we eat. So reefs also give people jobs and money.

Coral reefs are pretty. Many people like to visit reefs on vacation.

Coral reefs might even help doctors. They use reef animals to make medicines. These might cure people who are sick.

Reefs at Risk

Coral reefs do a lot for us. Yet we do not take care of them. In fact, we are harming them.

Lots of people catch fish from coral reefs. Sometimes people even blow up a reef. That makes it easier to catch fish. Yet it kills large parts of the reef.

Many people are also moving to areas near coral reefs. People make **pollution,** or harmful chemicals. The chemicals get into air, land, and water. This pollution can kill coral reefs.

Brain Damage. *Healthy (top) and unhealthy (bottom) brain coral show how pollution can affect reefs.*

Watery Wonderland. *A diver explores a reef near the Philippines. That is a country in Asia.*

Killing Coral

Today, pollution is hurting reefs. Some chemicals make coral polyps weak. The polyps get sick. Then many of them die.

Pollution can harm coral in other ways too. It can make some kinds of algae grow out of control. Soon the algae cover a coral reef. This kills coral polyps. Then the reef stops growing.

Pollution may also make ocean water warmer. If the water gets too warm, coral polyps lose their color. The reef turns a pale white.

Saving Coral Reefs

Can we save coral reefs? Many people think we can. We just need to work together. Helping coral means taking better care of our planet. We all need to do our part. Together we can save coral reefs—and our planet too.

WORDWISE

algae: tiny plants in the ocean

coral polyp: small ocean animal

coral reef: rock-like structure built by coral polyps

pollution: harmful chemicals that people make

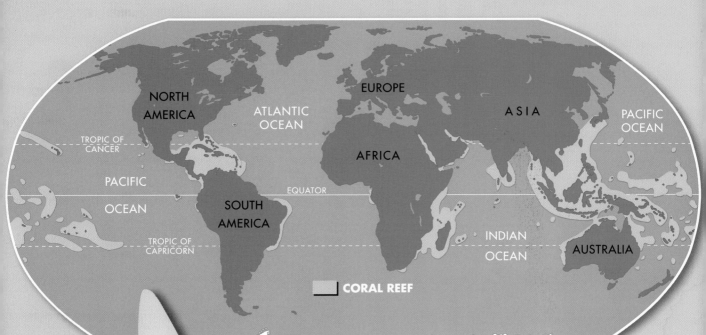

NORTH
AMERICA

EUROPE

ATLANTIC
OCEAN

ASIA

PACIFIC
OCEAN

TROPIC OF
CANCER

PACIFIC

AFRICA

OCEAN

EQUATOR

SOUTH
AMERICA

TROPIC OF
CAPRICORN

INDIAN

OCEAN

AUSTRALIA

CORAL REEF

ANTARCTICA

Coral
AROUND THE WORLD

Look at the map. It shows where many coral
reefs are found. Then read the facts below.
They tell why people need to protect coral reefs.

★ Coral reefs make up less than one percent of the area
in the world's oceans.

★ About ten percent of the world's food comes from
coral reefs.

★ Coral reefs protect the coastlines of 109 countries.
The reefs keep water from wearing away the land.

★ Twenty-five percent of ocean species, or kinds of plants
and animals, live in or around coral reefs.

★ About thirty percent of coral reefs may be killed or badly
hurt in the next ten years.

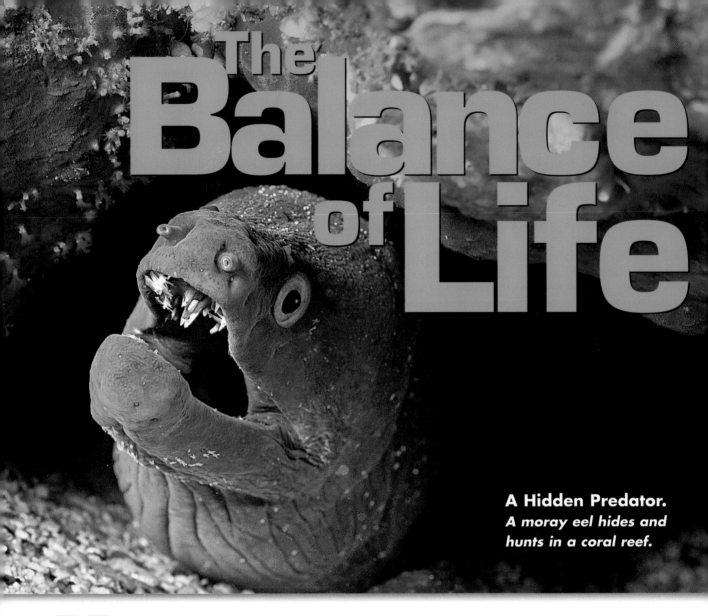

The Balance of Life

A Hidden Predator.
A moray eel hides and hunts in a coral reef.

Many plants and animals live in coral reefs. Reefs provide them with food. Reefs also give them shelter. Plants can find places to grow. Animals can find places to hunt and to hide.

All the living things in a coral reef depend on one another. They are all part of the balance of life. The coral reef helps them meet their needs.

Needing One Another

Life is not easy in a coral reef. Hungry animals are everywhere.

Some of them are predators. They eat other animals. Some animals are prey. They get eaten. Some are both. For example, a crab might eat a fish. It could then be eaten by an eel.

This is part of the balance of life in a reef. A crab needs fish. An eel needs crabs.

Coral Killer.
This sea star eats coral polyps.

A Taste for Wax

Many predators live in coral reefs. But most do not eat coral polyps. Why not? Polyps have wax in their bodies. Most animals cannot eat this wax.

But a few animals do not mind the polyp's wax. That is true for crown-of-thorns sea stars. These animals eat coral polyps—lots of them.

Fighting for Life

Sometimes the sea stars eat too many polyps. This can make the reef stop growing.

The crown-of-thorns sea star does not care if it hurts the reef. It is just hungry. The sea star is like most reef animals. It is only trying to meet its needs.

Eat or be eaten. That is the rule of the reef.

Partners for Life

Sometimes animals are partners. They help one another. That is what sea anemones and clownfish do.

These animals live together. The clownfish hides in the anemone's long, wavy arms. It chases away animals that eat anemones.

The anemone stings animals that eat clownfish. The clownfish and anemone help one another survive!

All for One, One for All

Reef animals survive in many ways. Some are partners. These animals help one another stay alive.

Some animals find other ways to meet their needs. They hunt alone. They look out for themselves.

Yet all of the living things in the reef depend on one another. They need each other to survive. They are part of the reef's balance of life.

Clowning Around. *A clownfish and a sea anemone are partners. They help each other survive.*

Coral Reefs

Dive into these questions to show what you know about coral reefs.

1 How do coral reefs form?

2 How do coral reefs help people?

3 Why are coral reefs in danger?

4 Name a predator that lives in a coral reef. What does it eat?

5 Name two reef animals that are partners. How do they help one another?